It Came From Outer Space

poems by

Carolina Morales

Finishing Line Press
Georgetown, Kentucky

It Came From Outer Space

*For my family
in memoriam and in continuum*

*This book is dedicated to C. Bursk,
a guiding star in the poetry galaxy.*

Copyright © 2018 by Carolina Morales
ISBN 978-1-63534-494-3 First Edition
All rights reserved under International and Pan-American Copyright Conventions. No part of this book may be reproduced in any manner whatsoever without written permission from the publisher, except in the case of brief quotations embodied in critical articles and reviews.

ACKNOWLEDGMENTS

I would like to thank the editors of the following journals in which versions of these poems have appeared:

Kelsey Review: "The Drama Queen speaks of her subjects", "Daguerreotype", "*Self-Portrait, Pregnant, NYC 1945*"
Latino Stuff Review: "*El Rey y Yo*"
Moonstone Anthology: "*Rings of Saturn*"
Nasty Women Poets: An Unapologetic Anthology of Subversive Verse: "To my eleventh draft"
Poetry South: "Blabbermouth Night at 'The Place' with Jack Spicer"
Spank the Carp: "A poem called Cliché"
Transcendent Visions: "Channeling my inner Bukowski", "*Ain't No Way to Treat a Lady*"
US1 Worksheets: "Translation", "*Sex and the City...*"

I would also like to thank the following individuals for their guidance and support: Christopher Bursk, Tim Craven, Anna Evans, Colby Cedar Smith, and my fellow workshop participants.

Special thanks also to Christen Kincaid, Leah and Kevin Maines, Christopher Bursk's master class and the Princeton Arts Council for their support.

Publisher: Leah Maines
Editor: Christen Kincaid
Cover Art: C. Dalmatian
Cover Design: Elizabeth Maines McCleavy

Printed in the USA on acid-free paper.
Order online: www.finishinglinepress.com
        also available on amazon.com

Author inquiries and mail orders:
Finishing Line Press
P. O. Box 1626
Georgetown, Kentucky 40324
U. S. A.

Table of Contents

I

Prologue—*Life on Mars* I 1
Rings of Saturn 2
Invasion of the Body Snatchers 3
The Outer Limits 4
Blabbermouth Night at 'The Place' with Jack Spicer 5
Frank O'Hara where are you tonight? 6
One upping Sharon Olds 8
Ay, Ay, Ai 9
Brief letter to a minor poet 10
To my eleventh draft 11
The Drama Queen speaks of her subjects 12
A poem named Trope 13
A poem called Cliché 14
Ain't No Way to Treat a Lady 15
Channeling my inner Bukowski 16

II

Translation 19
At the end of the workshop 20
Anatomy of a poem 21
Sex and the City, Season Three, Thirteenth Episode—
  Escape from New York 22
Honeymooners 23
Ode to an idol 24
El Rey y Yo 25
Waiting for Woody Allen—1963 26
Self-Portrait, Pregnant, NYC 1945 27
Daguerreotype 28
So 29
The War of the Worlds 30
Operation earth—the abduction 31
The Orangery 32
Epilogue—*Life on Mars* II 33

Language is a virus from outer space.

William S. Burroughs

When I write a line like 'A heart is true' it couldn't be more clichéd, and rhyming 'true' and 'you'—there could be no greater cliché. I don't have any trouble whatsoever with that. I don't operate by any external sense of what you can say and what you can't say.

Kay Ryan (on Tree Heart/True Heart)
Poets & Writers, Jan/Feb 2016

I

Prologue: *Life on Mars* I
    cento after Tracy K. Smith

The storm kicks up and nothing is ours.
    Downpour of days. Maps of fizzled stars.
        The great black distance. Clean lines
pointing only forward. Like some novels:
    Vast and unreadable. Language built from
        brick and bone. Relics of an outmoded design.
Our faulty eyes, our telltale heat, heart.

Ticking through our shirts. Weightless.
    Setting solid feet down on planets everywhere.
        Jupiter's vast canyons and seas. Lava strewn
plains and mountains. Packed in ice.
    The blank surface of the moon. Silent, buoyant,
        bizarrely benign. The word sun. Standard Uranium-
Neutralizing device. Its own quick span.

White noise. Like cellophane breaking. Molten,
    atomic, a conflagration of suns. So much
        for flags we bored into planets dry as chalk.
Image of the old planet taken from space.
    Blooming like a wound from the ocean floor.
        The night tide luminescent. And vague, swirls in,
and on and on. Complicit with gravity. Atlantis

buried under ice, gone one day from sight.
    Blunt ends of our fingers as we point.
        Not knowing a comet from a shooting star.
Jets blink. *Riding the earth Toward God-knows-*
    where. Dark matter. Like the space
        between people. The same wish that named
the planets. Knowing only the wish to know.

Rings of Saturn

flash their nothing
yellows, nothing
blues. Buried
bodies. Far above
earth. Pure vapor.
I spin and move.
Assigned to orbit
on a circular rack.
Into a nothingness.
A *beam me up*
space station.
A confession.
A moment
for truth.

appropriated from Marianne Baruch

Invasion of the Body Snatchers

There are those who dare travel beyond
barriers of place & time, dig the past
from its clenched grave, wear another's

name, zipper inside the other's flesh,
realign a spine with shifted backbone,
twist lips with projected words, crouch

behind another's vision from the vantage
of contemporary sight, fuel a fossil soul
with sensibilities of the now. For this

they can be lauded, praised for pirouettes
of imagination, bouts of empathy,
an arabesque of realizations sown

with arrogance, a bald irreverence
into pallid pod-like recreations.

The Outer Limits

As I read the winning poems,
I could hear their voices tick aloud,
louder than any human heartbeat.

Ba boom, ba boom. Ba ba ba boom!
In the aftermath, I envisioned
a field littered with spongy minds,

contracting and expanding inside
a hundred humongous heads signaling
their brain waves to the limits

of outer space where numbskull ideas hatch
and spiral to earth spawning a thousand
crazed mentees, thoughts bubbling

in secret labs where newly programmed
voices join forces to conquer the world.

Blabbermouth Night at 'The Place' with Jack Spicer

the poet who said he received poesy from
the dead—read their signals—followed
orders from beyond—took dictation from

satellite stations—transcribed outer realms,
who encouraged others to bleep noises—
broadcast disembodied voices—babble—

beam in "Martian" waves—push language
like furniture between material and invisible
worlds; this man gravitated by sorrows

and complications—later quarantined into
desolation—dismembered from his Berkeley
companions—self-exiled from his origins,

personal history, record of birth, as if born
through dislocation into a galaxy far from earth.

Frank O'Hara where are you tonight?

It is 9:00 p.m. I stand at a crosswalk.
The palm of the orange neon hand
stops me. Across the street, curtains
meet, tie back on either side a florescent
Psychic sign, tarot cards splayed
in the storefront window. To the right,
a plank—*Spiritual Healer & Advisor.*
Inside a woman tidies the room, dust
rag in hand, her dark hair twisted
and tied to the back of her head,
a crystal ball lifted and placed
on the chair beside her. Behind her
in a sleeveless T, a man with muscled
arms steers what appears to be a vacuum.

My dog tugs the leash. The silver
walking man releases me to an avenue
that leans in lamplight, flashes red
and green overhead, hesitates in amber.
Three doors over, the closed grocer
advertises Fish—*head to tail on sale,
two loaves for the price of one.* The liquor
store next door bargains wines and ales.
Behind a shuttered grill, the pharmacy
hides pills and potions, *Se Habla Español*
still blinking. The corner doctor's office
warns travelers from Africa's west
coast to check their coughs before
they enter. My dog and I pass

the neighbors' house where a wife
and daughters hang hijabs behind
closed doors. A Blessed Virgin,
in the attached row house, guards
the porch. In the home beside my own,
security warns *Smile you're on camera*
and I remind myself to avoid scratching
at my rear or adjusting my underwear
in the front garden. The stove-top lure
of *sofrito* seasons the air. Darkness tills
the bruised sky above us. A chill cuts
the warm. I go in, take up my pen, press
it to paper as we conjure our recipes
and charms against the scryer's storms.

One upping Sharon Olds
> ...when I was a child my parents
> tied me to a chair...
> S.O.

It's one thing to be tied
to a chair as a child
quite another to be tied
as a woman, each leg roped
to a wooden leg, hands bound
behind both backs or strapped,
arms onto arms of lumber,
duck tape sealing your voice
from air as if lips were a cushion
the mouth a tear, body stripped
to a slippery log, breasts hung
like milk laden fruit, head
bobbing, a branch
on an axe stricken tree

Ay, Ay, Ai

I read her poem about
you in which she calls
you out by name, words
beating your aging breasts,
aping your antecedents,
scratching a hairy hand
on your head; she,
who professes to admire
your work, aligns you
with a chimpanzee; she,
whose words peel
through stanzas heeled
in irreverence, politics,
clout, I leave her name out.

Brief letter to a minor poet
   for C.M.

Regurgitator of mumbo jumbo,
half truths, potions and spells,

promulgator of ideas as crinkled
bird nests of thought. *How many*

have formed, you ask, *since*
the world began? A sneer tugs

at the corner of your lip, *and still*
this world, and the same old shit!

Meanwhile, stockpiles of noirish
clichés click clack across

your sopping page. And tell me
what in heaven, in hell, on earth,

in this world possesses you,
in the first place, anyway.

To my eleventh draft

Nerve grinder, inept definer,

                       jive-time,
nickel and dime, two
       timin' rhymer,

this time, slimy little whiner,
                I'd like to kick

your behind,
         give you a shiner, slap

you flat into a binder,
    ship your butt to Indochina

but, somewhere inside,
   a patient,
             diligent writer resides,

     and I'm tryin' to find her.

The Drama Queen speaks of her subjects

So many I've aborted, abandoned
    on the kitchen table—misshapen,

incoherent, incomplete,
    imprisoned on a white sheet,

interrogated beneath
    the halogen lamp, slashed

and slashed again, stretched
    as on the rack, squeezed

as if between slabs of stone,
    crumpled, discarded for dead,

until my random return when
    one "I" looks into mine

and words beseech
    another chance.

A poem named Trope

This read is slant and lean,
   a brooding *papacito*

      in a tight, white T,
     for those who like 'em

muscled from the start,
    trimmed near the middle,

     poised by the end.
It's black leather zippered

  on a *bad* conceit, verse
    without a meter, a rebel

with a pause. It shifts
    to hold your attention,

stares you in the eyes,
    wants you not to look away.

A poem called Cliché

This poem
is a buxom blonde,
a hoochie mama in a tight
red dress. It's for those who
like 'em bustin' out the
top swayin' side to
side narrow
at the
waist, an hour-
glass figure slowly
runnin' out of sand. It's
askin' *Why don't you come
up & read me sometime?*
while lookin' for a big-
time spender.

Ain't No Way to Treat a Lady
after Helen Reddy

One rejection arrived in my inbox, no joke,
Christmas Eve. *Ho, ho,* hope the editors choked
on rotten candy canes. In the New Year,
I sent out, Sunday, to find my batch shot back,
Monday. *Hey, hey, hey,* did I neglect to say,
they mentioned a favorite they didn't accept.
Early in the Advent, a journal requested
I send in five more, all of which landed,
so to speak, on the cutting room floor. *Hee,
hee, hee,* woe is me. And I thought back
to my first acceptance sent postal in the Yuletide,
years ago, not the congrats for which I'd hoped,
just a yellow sticky note to apprise me of the one
they'd take. *Ha, ha, ha, fa la la la la…la…la…*

Channeling my inner Bukowski

Why do you write?
The instructor demanded,

her question arced
into a challenge, dotted

to a dare, as if our unspoken
answers already had failed.

Why do you write? She
repeated, arms folded

against us, brow arched,
eyes scalping the room,

lips tightened to a twitch
as I lowered my head

to mumble,
Cause I feel like it, bitch.

II

Translation

Even between speakers who share
the same tongue, so much

is misinterpretation—warnings taken
as threats, threats taken for jokes,

jokes taken with offense, our intentions
held hostage, gagged & bound, battered,

bruised beyond recognition. It's been
said that during a war, a bomb

dropped on foreign soil when one word
of a wired response was misunderstood.

As I sit at the kitchen table,
the language of your letters spread

before me on marked pages, ink leaks
onto my hand, the pen trembles.

At the end of the workshop

he held my poem by the edges

    with both hands
in the same manner another man

      might take a woman by the arms
before extracting a knife

    as adroitly as a pen

to slash a *cheek*,
          a *breast*,

a *hand*,
    a *thigh*,

        a *cunt*,
an argument, a repetition, a vein
    of thought, to bleed a page with ink

red as reams of blood

Anatomy of a poem
after Susan R.

The first poem
she presented
traced the shape
of a penis
while comparing
in fleshy details
a blow job
she'd given
to a hand job
she gave.
As I read
I envisioned
words
swelling
in her mouth
fingers
pressed on
the shaft
of a
pen
.

Sex and the City, Season Three, Thirteenth Episode—
Escape from New York

That racy foursome, Samantha, Carrie, Miranda,
Charlotte (taking leave of Trey), head for LA,
where, that vamp, Samantha, hooks a male
model-for-porno toys, cuts party chatter for
the grist of the matter, a twosome race straight
for his place. There, atop his bed, down to his thong,
the guy reveals his secret life—a published poet,
sheet at his feet, he stands to recite—*the leaves
blow up, the leaves blow down*...while Samantha
kneels in anticipation, squeals & claps for joy,
& for one tart/sweet empire moment our misguided
model believes he'll have it all—Samantha,
a move to the Apple—a new place to lay his head
& toot his horn for both his passions: poetry & porn.

Honeymooners
> *Pow! Zoom! Right in the kisser!*

You
raise
your
fist
to me
à la
R*al*ph
to *A*lice
lips
skewed
to one
side
promising
the moon

Ode to an idol

Old, obese, you drink your nights
in mansion halls, tenured whiskies,
rose vermouths, white Chablis, piles
of dirty clothes staggered against

the walls, a red sauce sliding above a plate
shattered on the Persian rug. I read it
in True Life magazine and remembered
when you were a god and I was a girl

letting myself in after school with a key to
the second floor, rear door apartment where
garter belts and pads cornered a broken
shelf. The wage earner's second dress bled

a soft red into the tub. A pipe leaked
a reddish rust behind the TV. There
the same movie aired seven days a week.
And in long summer days locked inside,

I remembered scene to scene, dialogues,
phrases, lines until you spoke a part
in my first literature. Our real lives beat
on in disappointment and disillusion. One

of my first was that I'd never bloom from
protruding ears and eye glasses to resemble
the exquisite beings you held in your arms,
a small price to pay for eyes that learned

to hear, ears taught to read, a heart pricked
to let red droplets. Now, in narrow halls,
red roses drift in place on papered walls.
Here, I feed from all that was given me.

El Rey y Yo

Born to this new spangled land,
I looked back for my past. We met.
You kissed my hand & tradition's
brocaded sleeve pulled me in. In
the beginning, I let you dress as brute
king. All the while I was Anna
gnawing, gnawing through your threads
& in the end your cuffs unraveled.
There could have been silk with gold
& silver weavings on your leaving.
But tangled in rage, frayed by confusion,
your long naked arm tore down
like a whip across the borrowed
blue, old & new of our oceans.

Watching for Woody Allen—1963

I waited for you at the club Monday night
& it was cookin', daddy-o, room tappin',

fingers snappin'. That was me at the corner
table in my little black dress, cigarette hangin'

from my lip, knee crossed, foot bobbin', shoe
dancin', just so, dangled from the toes while

the smooth horn wailed to the bongo's speech,
sax jivin' with the base, air fumin' blue heat,

all the crazy cats & blazin' chicks, hipsters
gathered like red trucks to a black fire. It was

smokin', man, though no one seemed to notice
the dark corners of the room curled in time's

white flames, as the band played on with that cool,
cool beat, & I waited, we all waited for you.

Self-Portrait, Pregnant, NYC 1945
after Diane Arbus

Years before my birth
        she poses in a mirror

hung on the back
        of her bedroom door,

composes her tawny stance,
        ripe breasted, melon

bellied, tilts a head crowned
        in thorn-brown hair,

balances along an angled
        cane, preens

her slender neck, cropped
        inside the frame,

camera, naked wall,
        bed already made.

Daguerreotype

Plated in brass, cushioned with
velvet, silvered on copper sheet,
embedded in ornamental Union
Case, his grey eyes stare from
a youthful face collared and
capped in Union garb, protected

by glass from a war fought
more than 100 years ago.

My bronze skin and dark hair
surface across the pale image
mirrored from my palm's lined
map, as slanted to the left, tilted
to the right, we reverse through
darkness, transpose into light.

So

Hitler was an artist, a painter,
not such a good one, but a creator
all the same. So his right hand,
Goebbel, was a philosopher,

a writer of poetry, novels, plays.
So their underling, Raabe,
was a composer, a conductor and
biographer for music's sake.

So the hands that labored seven
days and nights squeeze the creation
with a serpent's grip. So all our
blue-clear ideas and alpine inclusions

sound and crumble to dust, bleed
into pools of pigment and ink.

The War of the Worlds
original broadcast 1938

A red disc in yellowish/white, extra
    terrestrial light craters McGregor's
        field, Grover's Mill, New Jersey.
The quake of sound reverberates
    for miles around as the curious
        surround the site in a blurred flurry
of headlights, ignore authorities

who implore citizens to drive away.
    When the top of the craft rotates
        like a screw, pandemonium ensues.
Tripods rise from the pit spitting flames,
    march as walking war machines, burn
        the posted flag of truce, incinerate
denizens and troops, send black smoke

from the Marshes into Newark. Flash
    forward, present day, the State's governing
        city, twenty-two miles away, dashboards
alight like spaceship panels in a day-glow
    night. Sound systems pound a ground
        littered in fallout and decay. Bullets
ricochet. A rash of criminals stalk, attack.

Gang bangers clash in potholed, warzone
    streets. Copters chop the charcoal sky, ray
        an unearthly eye. Cop cars swirl blue/red
lights. Sirens wail their daily plight. Red
    engines shriek. White trucks cry as here
        and across our nation, cities sink
to the strains of a strange, terrestrial invasion.

Operation Earth—
the abduction

only his voice
as it orbits the room's
anatomy, its circular
theatre, words peeling

the soft fore
skin of our thoughts;
later, stationed
in the office, his eyes probe

our printed pages;
ears pressed
for feeble rhythms;
his pen, a scalpel

at the ready to inflict
its healing wounds

The Orangery

We are zestful little globes
packed inside a square crate
where windows arch floor
to ceiling flush with stars. A voice
floats through the microphone,
introduces the poet/guest, visitor
to our orchard, to our grove.

Words tilt like tiny moons,
circle from the maker's mouth
lighted by the spine of
a shepherding voice. Weightless
with expansion, we peel away
our pocked rinds, find the cheese
and rock at our fleshy cores.

Epilogue: *Life on Mars* **II**
    cento after Tracy K. Smith

We—flicker in. Radio waves from a generation
    ago. Marbled with static. Now audible,
        thrumming. Without a dial. Parallel
to what we know. Electronic screen. Clocks
    the minutes. *The last true man on this earth.*
        Charlton Heston is waiting to be let in.
Arms raised high, face an apocryphal white.

One man against a city of zombies. Our eyes
    adjust to the dark. What are they that move.
        The encumbrance of shadows? Hours plink
past like water from a window A/C.
    Some thin-hipped glittering Bowie-being—
        a Starman. Squinting through the dust.
Dragging a tail of white-hot matter. Vibrating

at the speed of belief. Bowing to the great stars
    that command, pitching stones. At whatever
        are their moons. Kubrick's 2001. Unfurls
in an aurora of orgasmic light. Opening wide,
    like a jungle orchid. The high beams of a million
        galaxies. Whisked across the wide-screen
of unparcelled time. We'll drift in the haze of space.

Like migratory souls. A momentary blip—.
    In those last scenes. That end at the end. Drifting
        to the edge of what doesn't end. The great
gleaming set goes black. Vast holy dark.
    Permeable like a mood. The others have come
        and gone. Storms through adjacent rooms.
A door punched through with light.

Carolina Morales is the author of four previous chapbooks of poetry, *Attack of the Fifty Foot Woman* (2015), *Dear Monster* (2012), *In Nancy Drew's Shadow* (2010), *Bride of Frankenstein and other poems* (2008). Her poems have been nominated for five Pushcart prizes and she is a past recipient of scholarships from summer programs at the Fine Arts Work Center in Provincetown, MA and the Artist/Teacher Institute, Rutgers-Camden, NJ along with honorable mentions for an Allen Ginsberg Award and a Mill Wills Fellowship. Her one-act plays have been produced/staged in California, New Jersey and Pennsylvania.

www.ingramcontent.com/pod-product-compliance
Lightning Source LLC
LaVergne TN
LVHW041555070426
835507LV00011B/1100